The more unusual chocolate-coloured members of the breed

those wishing to own a no-nonsense dog, who is loyal and trustworthy with children and is so much fun. Labradors can become lap dogs if you let them, sleeping on top of your bed, or simply finding somewhere near you to relax, enjoying your company.

The Labrador has a kind, intelligent expression, is strongly built, very active, broad across the skull, broad and deep through the chest and ribs and broad and strong over the loins and hindquarters. The Labrador has a unique tail which is described as an 'otter's tail'; it is thick at the base, tapering gradually to the tip with a rounded appearance and no feathering. All this seems to describe a sensible type but the Labrador can be a real handful when grow-

ing up; he enjoys a good chew on whatever is available and will enjoy giving his family a lot of cheek. His love of attention enables him to be given the basic training at a young age helping him to grow into a well-behaved adult. He can be trained to sit, give paws, wait for his dinner, fetch his favourite toy for you and, if you are very lucky, be house trained in a few weeks. Throughout his long life (perhaps twelve to sixteen years) the Labrador's tail is usually wagging so it is also used to knock over cups and ornaments on coffee tables, bang against your legs and knock incessantly against walls. Labradors are happy dogs.

Labradors are the ideal family pet: they enjoy a lot of exercise when mature, love

Taking part in a fun day

water and retrieving. An active, fit Labrador is the ideal companion for a teenager to have fun with. If you have access to open public spaces or live near a beach where dogs are allowed, a Labrador can give hours of enjoyment. They are also the ideal dogs for older people who have been told to walk to improve their health; they are robust, require just a little attention to their coat, are generally very good eaters, just love being petted and very few people are afraid of them. They should

Well retrieved with a soft mouth not crushing the ball

THE
LABRADOR RETRIEVER

CONTENTS

BREED CHARACTERISTICS

The Labrador Retriever is of medium size, good looking, and a multi-purpose dog used for a variety of activities including: family pet, guide dog for the blind, sniffer dog for drugs and explosives and working gundog who is especially good in water. He is also a great favourite at dog shows. With his steady character, gentle manner and intelligence the Labrador is ideal for all these pursuits. The Labrador comes in three colours: black, yellow and liver (chocolate). The term 'Golden Labrador' is incorrect according to the Kennel Club although many people often use that description. In my travels all over the world judging the breed I am constantly amazed at how they have caught the attention of dog lovers. In almost every country they draw huge entries at dog shows. This is the breed for

Labradors are often used as guide dogs for the blind

Cindy shows the kind, intelligent expression typical of the breed

never be bought as guard dogs. They have been bred to have soft mouths and to be good mixers with other dogs and people. They love children but remember to introduce young Labradors carefully to very young children as they can be rather too exuberant and knock them over.

They are called Labradors as they were developed from dogs brought over to Britain from Canada by English fishermen who worked the seas off Newfoundland in the nineteenth century. Careful selection by the landed gentry, who developed the dogs' instinct to retrieve fish which had fallen overboard from the fishing vessels anchored in the harbours, ensured they have become the most successful of all the retrieving breeds. Watch out if there is water about, your Labrador will be sure to paddle through it! It is the dog selected by many famous people as their companion and Her Majesty The Queen, owner of the Sandringham Labradors, is Patron of The Labrador Retriever Club. Another prominent owner is the President of the United States of America, Bill Clinton, the proud owner of Buddy, a lively chocolate dog who is obviously trained not to jump up when greeting his master.

Labradors love being outdoors in all sorts of weather

CHOICE OF PUPPY

Choosing your Labrador puppy should always begin with reputable breeders. I recommend using a Labrador breed club list. The people on these lists breed from sound, good-natured Labradors and are generally very experienced. Both parents should be X-rayed for hip dysplasia through the Kennel Club/British Veterinary Association scheme and preferably be below the breed average score. At the moment the average is sixteen. The best possible score is 0-0. Hip dysplasia is common to all heavy-boned dogs and some smaller, lighter breeds. The hip joint is badly formed, causing a painful and debilitating arthritic condition that affects movement, especially as the Labrador ages. It can be operated on in the more serious cases but this is expensive and not always successful.

Eyes too can be affected by various diseases and you should ensure that the breeder takes part in the yearly eye examinations by specially qualified veterinarians and that you can inspect the certificates available to prove the eyes are clear.

If you cannot decide which puppy to select from the litter tell the breeder the characteristics you require in a dog. You may like them to be very active or you may prefer a quieter pup, you may like the

Veyatie Paddywack, aged fifteen, with his great-great-grandchildren

This five-week-old bitch has spotted something interesting

biggest pup in the litter, or perhaps the smallest one. Do not, however, choose a nervous, frightened puppy. It will always be that way and, consequently, will be untrustworthy. Nervous puppies are generally the ones that bite (this applies to all breeds).

It should be possible to see the mother of the puppies. Observe her temperament and see if she meets your requirements in looks and character but do remember that she will not be at her best having just weaned a litter of greedy puppies; her coat will be falling out and she may be thin. The sire may live hundreds of miles away so do not be too suspicious if he is not on the premises. If the breeder has travelled many miles to use him it can be a sign the litter has been bred with great care. Beware a breeder who breeds many types of dogs. Never buy from a puppy farm.

Show Champion Midnight Mystery and Fullwell Free-booter at Halshimoor whc also became a Champion

Yellows vary from foxy red to pale cream. June is as pale as they ever are

This yellow is a deeper shade and very attractive

COLOUR

Colour plays no part in the character of a Labrador, so it is just a matter of personal choice. Yellows come in a wide range of shades from pale cream to foxy red but should, perhaps, be avoided by those who are extremely house proud or who frequently wear dark clothes. They do not lose their coat more frequently than blacks or chocolates but those yellow dog hairs really do stand out on dark surfaces and clothes. Chocolate coats can fade in bright sunshine giving a mottled, patchy look part of the year, and the eye colour is sometimes rather light yellow giving a hard expression which is something a Labrador should never have. They are often more expensive than the other colours because there are fewer of them and demand for a scarcer Labrador pushes the price up. How lucky you are to have three colours to choose from!

Flanders Pride from Belgium is a good example of a black

Chocolate is a popular colour. The eyes have a tendency to light yellow but Rusty has a lovely eye colour

DOG OR BITCH

Bitches tend to remain closer to home than males, content in many cases to go to the edge of your property and enjoying the attention from your neighbours with no inclination to roam for miles on their own. Labrador males will wander off more readily scenting the air for girlfriends and marking their territory very frequently, so you will need a well-fenced back garden! As their sense of smell is very acute they can scent a girlfriend many miles away. When in season, bitches present a slight problem. The first season generally comes at about ten months of age then around six months thereafter. The indoor kennel comes in very handy during seasons ensuring the bitch cannot escape looking for a mate, especially if the children continually leave the outside door open. Spaying, if desired, should be done midway between the first and second seasons and, after the operation, you must watch her weight. Dogs are slightly bigger and stronger than bitches but if well trained when young make wonderful companions.

Cindy at a show in South Africa waiting patiently for her master

Fabracken Ocean Breeze, black dog aged two

Yellow puppies Rosie and Ted aged five weeks

Buying an Older Labrador

Many people prefer to purchase an older Labrador rather than taking on the task of rearing a puppy. Over the years many Labrador breeder friends have rehomed older Labradors very successfully giving great pleasure to their new owners, many of whom have perhaps lost their old favourite and are pining for the company an older Labrador gives. It does not take long for the Labrador to appreciate their new owners, love for them. Even kennel Labradors that have not quite got to the top in the show ring make ideal pets, quickly becoming house trained and devoted to their owners. A trial period is usually agreed with this type of purchase.

- Remember when you buy from a reputable breeder advice is only a phone call away.

Feeding

Today the choice of suitable foods for your Labrador puppy is enormous. The range of dog foods on sale in most good pet stores, supermarkets and veterinary surgeries ensures quality dog food that is easily available to the general public.

The breeder should supply you with a diet sheet suitable for at least a year. Diet is important in the formation of bones and incorrect feeding can increase the Labrador's chances of developing hip dysplasia, rickets and other bone-related problems. Follow the feeding instructions carefully. Do not overfeed; give small meals spread evenly over the day. When you first take your puppy home make sure his food is as fed by the breeder. Good breeders will give you some food to take home with you, or perhaps sell you a big bag to ensure he is fed the right food for his age. The feeding will change as he grows up. First he will be fed puppy grade until about six months when he should progress to junior grade of the same product, then, when he is around twelve months, change to an adult grade. Feed the quantity as directed and with the number of feeds decreasing as he grows from four or five to eventually one meal a day. Or you may prefer to give two small meals a day.

Fabracken Name in Lights at six weeks

Today 'complete' foods are very popular and are readily available. This type of food has all the nutrients and vitamins your puppy requires to grow up correctly and soundly. Do not add extra meat, minerals or vitamins as the food has been carefully designed to give the puppy everything required for correct development. Sometimes a spoonful of tinned food in the complete food is necessary for a short time to encourage slow eaters to acquire the taste for complete food but should not be added on a long-term basis. Tinned foods are also good but require a mixer to be fed simultaneously. Always provide readily available, fresh drinking water at all times. If you wish to change your puppy's diet, do so gradually so as to avoid stomach upsets. A little of the new, a little of the old until gradually the diet is changed without harming your puppy.

STURDY NOT FAT

When you go to the vet for your puppy's first inoculation you will probably be told he is too fat. Vets always think Labradors are too fat. It is possibly a warning not to let your puppy become a fat adult. I believe a Labrador puppy should be rounded. The description of a Labrador is 'strongly built, broad and deep through chest and ribs' and if you do not want a dog of that description a Whippet, Jack Russell Terrier or some other light-bodied dog might be more suitable for you. By all means listen to the vet but as a breeder and exhibitor who has also worked Labradors I maintain he should be a sturdy, well-boned, barrel-ribbed active dog with plenty of muscle. However, there is a world of difference between a well-built Labrador and a fat one.

Many people love Labradors so much that they keep as many as possible

GROOMING

What a fortunate dog owner you are! Owning a Labrador means you have very little grooming to do. In more than thirty-five years in Labradors we have used only four grooming aids – a towel, a damp chamois, a coat stripper and a velvet glove. Not for you the dread of having to take him out when it is wet returning with a heavily matted, soaking coat to dry, comb out, cut away tangles, or having to pay expensive grooming bills every few months to keep him looking good. After a walk in muddy conditions, a quick rub down with a towel, then finished with the chamois dries and cleans your Labrador allowing him to rub against your furniture with no chance of any dirt coming off his coat. When he is casting his coat the stripper takes away much of the loose hair. Doing this each day for a few minutes will keep him looking decent. The velvet glove really puts a shine on a black

Blues Singer at Brigburn (*left*) and Ch. Fabracken Meadow Mint (*right*) showing their magnificent condition

The kind faces of this group illustrate the breed's good nature

Labrador and the dog loves the sensation of your hands grooming him. Grooming on a regular basis maintains contact between owner and dog and gives good control over the Labrador without an obvious lesson. Remember, grooming gives you the first insight into any skin or body problems, with your hands feeling any lumps or cuts not immediately seen by the eye. As the Labrador has a double coat consisting of a longer, oily, hard top coat over a dense undercoat he excels in water. His ribs remain dry, ensuring he is happy in conditions when some other breeds are miserable.

TRAINING

Training your Labrador should be fun. The best training is when your puppy does not know he is being trained. In other words do not let bad habits form. For example when he is playing with his toy or a chew take this away from him on regular occasions saying 'good boy'. Give it back to him quite quickly and he will soon learn never to snap at anyone taking his chew or toy. Never feed bones, especially chicken bones, as most blockages to the intestines and damage to teeth come from bones. Give your Labrador hide chews or tasty sterilised manufactured bones.

Rossbank Jill at five weeks…

LEAD TRAINING

When lead training, use a very short lead. I use a slip lead made from rope or nylon. If you buy a long lead and allow the puppy to walk ahead of you he will always want to pull you. Keep the Labrador's head in line with your left knee. Hold the lead in your right hand with your left hand mid-way up the lead, gently pulling the puppy back when he goes beyond your knee. If you start this way, your children and their grandparents will be able to walk the grown Labrador without fear of being pulled off their feet. Ensure your Labrador is fitted with a collar and identity tag when leaving your property.

… enjoying a chewy slipper which is safe and tasty

Ready for training; note the slip leads which give good control and do not hurt the dog

Tom is controlled with a gentle pull on his slip lead to keep him level with his handler's knee

EXERCISE

Short walks are essential. Think of your Labrador puppy as a baby. How far would you walk a little child? Hips must not be overworked and that means controlled exercise in your back garden with no fast running after balls, sticks, or playing with agile adult dogs. Exercise him with great caution for the first twelve months and you will dramatically increase the chances of having a healthy adult Labrador. Time goes by quickly and soon the Labrador will be able to run and jump to his heart's content. This more disciplined exercise also gives you an older Labrador that will look for you when off the lead for free exercise happy to come back to you when called.

Walking correctly at heel

'SIT' TRAINING

Sitting at your command can also be taught when he is very young. Line the Labrador puppy up beside you with his head at your knee and place one hand on his hips pressing down with the other on his neck pulling upwards. Always praise him. When putting his dinner out, make the puppy wait for a short time looking at your hands holding his meal and tell him to 'sit'. When going for a walk, again, tell him to sit then put the lead on his collar.

CHEWING

Never give him a slipper or an old shoe to chew. When he grows up he will think he is allowed to chew good slippers and shoes! Buy him a toy big enough not to be swallowed and strong enough not to be ripped apart. His teeth will be very busy for perhaps twelve months so give him a good supply of chews daily. Many of these chews are designed to clean your dog's teeth while he is enjoying his chew and pet stores have a very good selection.

Sitting at heel

Four-month-old Flora sits to command – but not for long

He can't swallow this ball; never give toys which can be swallowed

TRAINING CLASSES

Some vets hold puppy socialising classes and these can be most enjoyable. When you feel you would like to go further with your Labrador's training contact your local dog training class. Veterinary surgeons generally have these training clubs listed on their notice boards. The trainers are usually very sympathetic to the novice owner and the classes can be very good for socialising your Labrador, and you. If you are interested in gundog training seek out a local gundog club or Labrador breed club and take their advice.

Teaching Ben to sit at just three-and-a-half months

Heidi and Jet are easy to walk on their slip chains

SOFT MOUTHS

It is essential for Labradors to have soft mouths, particularly if used for gundog work. A puppy's soft mouth can be maintained by not encouraging him to indulge in pulling games with an object held in your hands and the puppy's mouth. This type of game also encourages possessiveness.

PUPPIES AND CHILDREN

When a puppy plays using his teeth he can frighten children because his teeth are very sharp at that age. If you find he is rather rough with his teeth, take his lips and gently squeeze his sharp eye teeth into them, letting him know he should not bite so hard. He will give a little squeal but will soon learn how far he can go. This must be done just after he has been

naughty. Never reprimand a dog long after the naughty deed is done, he will be confused about what he has done. One should never, of course, leave a baby in the room alone with any dog. Play safe, do not take risks with a child.

Remember that your Labrador puppy gets tired frequently, just like a baby, so when he wants to sleep, tell the children to leave him till he wakes.

HOUSE TRAINING

As soon as the puppy wakes up lead him into the garden, always to the same spot, and wait till he relieves himself, then bring him in with words of praise. With luck he will quickly become house trained. If he is regularly put outside till he performs, he will gradually learn to be clean inside.

INDOOR KENNELS

If you want to go out for a while and not worry about your furniture being chewed, I strongly recommend buying an indoor kennel. These are used by many dog breeders all over the world. It becomes the puppy's bed and safe area. When he is in his indoor kennel, teach the children that that is his resting place and he is not to be disturbed till he awakens. The kennels fold down and can be taken to friends' homes and erected in minutes so that the puppy can enjoy being with you. They fit in many cars thus saving expensive repairs to electric wiring and roof linings, seats, etc. They are worth the money especially if you buy one suitable for an adult Labrador, so that the puppy has a bed for life.

Indoor kennel; these are well worth the expense and are long lasting

Young yellows wishing they could get over the fence

HEALTH CARE

Accidents will happen but try to avoid the obvious ones: do not buy small toys, they invariably end up in the Labrador's stomach; do not leave medicines lying about or let your Labrador out in the garden if you have used slug pellets, they are extremely dangerous when swallowed; never let him off the lead near a road, he may be the best-trained Labrador but if he smells a bitch in season he will not respond to your wishes; human chocolate is very

A good example of a yellow bitch

Labradors have double coats which allows them to cope with very cold conditions

Black bitch Maggie aged three

toxic to dogs if eaten in large quantities, he should be given only dog chocolate bought from pet suppliers.

If he is off colour take him to the vet for a check up. Nowadays many dog owners take out pet insurance, usually continuing with that supplied by the breeder which may be for three months.

WORMING

Frequent worming is essential. The puppy should have been on a worming programme when purchased. Thereafter a six-monthly routine with pills supplied by the vet is a must. The dog's worming programme is also essential for children's health, their eyes being particularly vulnerable to parasitic infection. Proper worming eradicates this danger as does the practice of disposing of your dog's faeces. Always carry a scooper when walking the dog and, immediately he defecates, pick it up and put it into a suitable bin. Public parks where dogs are still allowed generally provide these bins.

TEETH

Regular dental care prevents bad breath, tooth decay and gum diseases such as epulides where the gum grows around and above the teeth with risk of gum infection. Severe cases of epulides can require surgery to remove excess gum. Always use special

Maggie wants to know if she should bring the ball back!

dog toothpaste to clean a dog's teeth as human toothpaste is unsuitable. You can buy this from your veterinary surgeon or pet store. You will also need a dog toothbrush or rubber cleaning pad which fits over your finger. Your Labrador will soon get used to the sensation and enjoy having his teeth cleaned. There are also dog treats that are designed to clean the teeth and can be fed as a training reward throughout the day ensuring your dog remains in good dental health.

EARS

As in other breeds some Labradors develop severe ear problems if they are not checked regularly. Using cotton wool, about once a week gently clean with ear cleaner. Touching and cleaning will help you develop a good relationship with your Labrador who will enjoy the attention.

Two yellows from South Africa

TAKING HIS TEMPERATURE

The normal temperature of a dog is 101.5 °F. His temperature can be tested by putting a thermometer one-and-a-half inches (approx. four centimetres) into his anal canal for a minute although you should ask a vet to show you how to do this.

FIRST-AID KIT

It is advisable to have a small first-aid kit and this should contain:

- A stock of bandages, crepe and cotton
- Ear drops
- Tape for securing bandages
- Cotton wool

- Thermometer
- Antiseptic cream

If you are in any doubt about your Labrador's health, consult your vet.

Mixing dogs with other animals should be done carefully until they trust and know each other

Twelve-year-old Kelly relaxing… and with feline friend

USEFUL ADDRESSES

For details of Labrador Breed Clubs in
your area contact:
The Kennel Club
1 Clarges Street,
London W1Y 8AB
Telephone 0870 606 6750

In America contact:
The American Kennel Club
4th Floor,
260 Madison Avenue,
New York NY 10016/2401

In Germany contact:
**Verband fur das Deutsche Hundewesen
(VDH)**
Westfalendamm 174,
44141 Dortmund,
Germany

ACKNOWLEDGEMENTS

The author is most grateful to the following for permission to reproduce photographs in this book: John D. Jackson, Mrs J. Rawlinson, Messrs J. & M. Rawlinson, M. Roovers-Smet and Anne Taylor.

British Library Cataloguing-in-Publication Data.
A catalogue record for this book is available from the British Library

ISBN 0.85131.776.6

Published in Great Britain in 2000 by
J. A. Allen an imprint of Robert Hale Ltd.,
Clerkenwell House, 45–47 Clerkenwell Green,
London EC1R 0HT

Series design Paul Saunders, layout by Terence Caven
Series editor John Beaton
Colour processing by Tenon & Polert Colour Scanning Ltd., Hong Kong
Printed in Hong Kong by Dah Hua International Printing Press Co. Ltd.